GRANT WRITING FOR COMPLETE BEGINNERS

The Ultimate Guide on How to Learn and Master How to Write Grant Proposal from Beginners to Pro

Ramon Tibbs
Copyright@2022

D1013914

TABLE OF CONTENT

CHAPTER 1

INTRODUCTION

The submission of a grant request should be viewed as the beginning of a project that will culminate in a measurable deliverable or other result. In order to receive financing, projects have to demonstrate that they have produced measurable outcomes. A grant proposal that has been well written, organized, and presented has a far better chance of being awarded the grant.

CHAPTER 2

In that case, what exactly is a grant proposal?

In a nutshell, it's a request for capital to be invested in a venture, whether it be for profit or not. At first look, it may appear that grant applications are primarily beneficial to the company or individual entrepreneur who is in need of financial assistance. However, that is not entirely accurate.

It is not an investment in any random project, but rather an investment in a project that will result in a good change for the grantee (a grantee is an individual or organization that gives you the money). As a result, they have the potential

to have a significant influence
on matters that relate to the
ethics, values, or culture of an
organization.

A few quick statistics:

More than one hundred distinct
categories of government grants
are made available for
application by non-profit
organizations through the
Department of Health and
Human Services. One such
example is the Federal Grant
A8201, which is a program that
focuses on preventative
initiatives such as decreasing
the use of tobacco among kids
and giving information about
good eating habits across the
United States.

A single application for a government grant can take an average nonprofit organization up to two hundred hours to write. That is a significant time commitment for any business, but by using the PandaDoc grant application template, you may shave off as much as 30 hours of that time commitment. The benefits can be substantial as well: Each year, the United States federal government donates $3 billion in grants, and it has guaranteed funding rates that have never been seen before of over 50 percent for this budget cycle!

If you are seeking for a means to increase the success of your nonprofit organization, the solution can be found in the statistic shown below. 75% of grant applicants who filed an application were successful in winning an award, while 94% of grant applicants who had applied for three to five awards were successful in winning at least one! 98 percent of candidates who had six or ten applications in hand were eligible for this promotion.

CHAPTER 3

HOW TO WRITE A GRANT PROPOSAL STEP BY STEP

The essential processes involved in writing an excellent grant proposal

You have to get everything ready before you start. If we are discussing how to draft a grant application for a non-profit organization, then you should consider this document to be a very minor component of your overall fundraising strategy.

To begin, you will need to determine your objectives for the fundraising effort, formulate a cost estimate, create a timetable for the project, and search for potential funding.

The question "how to draft a grant proposal for a small business" follows a method that is almost exactly the same. Prior to submitting a grant application in the United States of America, a new firm must first get registered in a government grant program.

To save yourself some time and effort, you should send in a brief grant letter before completing a comprehensive grant request.

In the event that your Grantee agrees with the contents of your letter and sends you a request for a formal grant proposal, you are free to move through with the process of producing a thorough RFP response to this potential investor.

You can do this challenging process with the help of our document management software, which may save you even more time and get the job done more quickly. Besides grant proposals, it can handle your quotations, agreements, contracts, and proposals.

Let's move on to the format of a typical grant proposal, which you need to stick to in order to be successful.

First, draft an impressive application cover letter.

Your cover letter is the ideal chance to attract the attention of the funder and begin the process of building a relationship with them. The letter, in contrast to the remainder of your grant application, might be written in a less official tone and addressed more directly to the reader.

Your cover letter should primarily serve the purpose of persuading the reader to continue reading your proposal. They have probably received tens or even hundreds of grant applications, and your letter should differentiate you as much as possible from the throng in order to increase your chances of being selected.

When it comes to cover letters, the following is a list of things that should and should not be done:

Do:

Keep it brief: the maximum allowed is three to four paragraphs. Directly declare what it is that you want to do at the outset, and get to the point as fast as possible.

Say what it is that you require: Mention how much money you need right off the beginning, as well as the purpose of the funds. You should not be scared to be straightforward; the reader should be aware that you are qualified for this award.

To avoid sounding like a broken record, this is not the place to just restate what you mentioned in the proposal. You are permitted to deviate somewhat from the topic at hand and yet contribute something of worth.

Bring together the following: Demonstrate that you have an understanding of the funder and that you can clearly connect their objective and the cash they provide to your planned project.

Don't:

You shouldn't create a sentimental tale about your company or purpose since it will make you sound overly emotional. Convey your message in a style that is less formal, but be sure to keep the emphasis on your ideas throughout.

Mention those who are competing against you; there is no need to evaluate yourself in relation to others. You should just emphasize your own intended objective and work hard to generate a positive first impression without bringing up anyone else.

The following is an example of a strong opening to a cover letter:

Sincerely, Mr. Jones,

The Pet Care Clinic humbly submits a request for a grant in the amount of $30,000 in order to support the South Boston Health Center Project.

We are aware of the issues that pet owners in our service region encounter because our hospital is the biggest independently owned veterinary facility in the Boston area. Given that South Boston has the highest population density of pets in comparison to other parts of the city, we are especially concerned about the poor quality of service that is provided there.

By the end of the year 2021, we are determined to find a solution to this problem by expanding the size of our community and making our knowledge and experience available to the people and animals of Boston. As a result of the South Boston Health Center Project, we will be able to give access to...

Straight to the point, with no filler words!

The second step is to begin with a concise executive summary.

Moving on to the process of writing grants, every successful grant application should begin with a concise executive summary.

An executive summary is simply a condensed description of the full proposal; this type of summary is also known as a proposal summary. It presents your firm, market sector, proposal, project aims – effectively, your grant request.

It must to include an adequate amount of depth and specifics, and it ought to be pragmatic and accurate. Get to the point as swiftly as possible.

Do: Limit its length to no more than two pages: You must supply the grantee with exactly the right amount of information so that they may read only this section and still have a good understanding of who you are and why you want funding.

Please include the following resources: Mention the money that you are asking and provide a condensed explanation of the spending strategy that you intend to use for those dollars.

Please tell us about your organization: Do not be hesitant to inform the grantee about your organization's history, mission, and goals; despite the fact that you will go into further depth about this topic later on.

Don't: Communicate with the funder on a personal level: The cover letter is the sole place to include this information. Now that we have begun drafting a grant proposal, it is time to take things in a more serious direction.

Give away an excessive amount: Don't go into too much detail about the project description just now; there will be time for that later.

Therefore, the following are some questions that will be answered by a skilled grant writer in their executive summary:

1. What is your organization's goal and background? What do you do?

2. What is the name of your project, and who exactly is it intended to assist?

3. What issue are you attempting to resolve, and why should others care?

4. What is your ultimate objective, and how will you determine whether or not you have accomplished it?

5. For what reason should you be given the money? What exactly are your areas of expertise?

6. How much money do you require to complete the project, and how do you intend to

finance it in the future? Do you
have access to any other
sources of funding?

Step 3: Present your company
or organization

You are now able to begin with
your company or organization
since you have successfully
established the context for the
entire presentation. It would be
helpful if you could share as
much pertinent information as
possible about your
organization's history, mission,
experience, and so on.

In this section, you will
showcase your organization's
competence by including a
biography of each important

member of staff, your company's track record in business (success stories), corporate goals, and philosophy.

Recommendations from previous customers, letters of gratitude, and comments from both customers and the wider public are required pieces of writing for a grant submission.

Include particulars on any current industry certifications (such as ISO or Quality Certifications), licenses, as well as business and indemnity insurance policies, if applicable.

You need to demonstrate that your company or organization has the capacity and ability to meet all deliverables from both an execution perspective as well as meet all legal, safety, and quality obligations. Specifically, you need to show that your company or organization has the capacity to meet all quality obligations.

In order to demonstrate that you are able to fulfill your financial obligations to your workers and contractors, it is possible that you may be required to present solvency statements.

Do:

Maintain your objectivity. It's tempting to start congratulating yourself a bit too much and trying to convince the people

who are reviewing your grant
application that you're the best
of the best. Stay on the straight
and narrow and avoid falling
into this trap.

Give some background
information, such as when and
why the firm or organization
was established. Make an effort
to connect your purpose with
that of the organization that is
giving you the funding in the
most natural way possible.

Don't:

You are providing too much
detail; for example, there is no
requirement that you disclose
the names of all of your
workers. Include short

biographies of important members of staff (such as the executive director), and simply state the overall number of employees you have.

Abandon the main point: The entirety of this part need to be written in such a way as to prove that your organization is superior than all others in terms of its ability to receive financing. Be careful not to go overly verbose and overlook this important detail.

Step 4. Write a direct problem statement

The issue statement is one of the most essential components

25

of the overall framework of the grant proposal.

This section, which may also be referred to as the "needs statement" or the "statement of need," is the spot where you describe why an issue exists in your community

You may be required to conduct significant study on the background of the underlying problem, past solutions that were attempted and may have been unsuccessful, and an explanation of why your solution would make a difference in the world.

The issue statement in a grant proposal that is likely to be successful will place a heavy emphasis on quantitative data and provide an unmistakable illustration of how your company fulfills a need.

Do:

Use comparable data: Put your faith in the outcomes that other communities have achieved after putting your idea into action and finding it to be satisfying.

Emphasize the sense of urgency, emphasizing how important it is to get started on this project as soon as possible rather than delaying it.

Keep your attention on the primary issue at hand and do

your best not to let it divert to other occurrences that may be playing a role in the primary issue that you are attempting to solve.

Don't:

Make it about you: The financing for the grant is not needed by your organization; rather, it is needed for the community.

Employ logic that is circular: Don't approach the issue by saying, "The city doesn't have a youth center –> We can create a youth center," since that's not the right approach. Why is it even necessary for the city to have a youth center in the first place? This idea ought to serve as the driving force behind your writing process.

5. Specify both your short-term and long-term aims

The process of writing a grant proposal includes clearly outlining your aims and objectives, which is another key element of the process. In point of fact, a significant number of projects are rejected because the people behind them forget about or botch this phase, meaning that all of their labor is in vain.

Write out specifics on the target goal as well as the criteria that will be used to evaluate the project's success. This part is essential for giving information on the advantages that the grantee, community, government, or client will receive as a result of their investment in the project.

In addition, although the terms goals and objectives are sometimes used interchangeably, they should be kept distinct. Think of goals as broad statements, and objectives as statements of purpose that are more detailed, with quantifiable results and a time limit attached to them.

Do:

Define outcomes as objectives: an aim is something you want to attain; it is not something you want to do.

Be sure that your goals are SMART: If your goals aren't SMART, it will be impossible for you to accurately measure your progress: SMART goals are ones that are Specified, Measurable, Achievable, Realistic, and Time-bound.

Establish a connection between the aims and objectives and the audience: Your project's end outcome should always be the improvement of your community as measured in some way, and this improvement should be measurable.

Don't:

Achieve more than you should: Be sure that you can achieve

your goals, and don't get too far ahead of yourself in the process.

Confusion between procedures and goals: Goals are never articulated in the form of processes but rather always as results and quantifiable outputs together with a deadline.

The following is an illustration of some effectively worded goals and objectives.

The youngsters who attend schools located inside the [village] will have their literacy and general ability to express themselves improved as the goal of this project.

Reading and writing exam scores for fourth-graders in the [community] are now at an average of 55 out of 100 points. The goal is to raise these scores by at least 20 percent by the end of the 2023 school year.

Take note of the goal's more upbeat and general tone, in contrast to the objective, which is more quantifiable and gets straight to the point.

6. The design of the project, including its techniques and tactics

Now that the funding agency or grantee is aware of your objectives, it is important to describe your strategy for accomplishing those objectives to them.

Make a list of the new personnel and talents, extra facilities, transport, and support services that you require in order to successfully complete the project and achieve the predefined success indicators.

Maintaining a proper focus on the tasks, deliverables, and results of the project requires a good level of discipline and methodology in project management, as well as the specification of comprehensive requirements and the articulation of individual activities within the project timeline.

Do:

Maintain a connection to the goals: It is essential that the techniques and tactics you employ maintain a connection not just to the requirements statement but also to the goals that you have stated.

Provide examples: Find past projects where the same tactics were used and found to be successful, if at all possible.

Show that the benefits outweigh the costs: Make certain that the person who awards grants is aware that the approaches you choose are logical, supported by ample research, and efficient users of resources.

Don't:

Assume the following: Don't approach the themes as though

the reader already has extensive knowledge of the subject. Be as descriptive as possible and explain how your approaches work as though you were speaking to someone who had no prior knowledge of your business or proposals.

Forget about your audience: You will need to provide evidence to show that the tactics you have selected are appropriate for the community in question.

Step 7: The assessment section: keeping tabs on your progress

Evaluation of the process is discussed in this part; specifically, how will you monitor the development of your program?

It also covers the required amount of time for the assessment, as well as the individuals who will conduct the evaluation, as well as the particular abilities or goods that will be required, as well as the total cost of the evaluation phase of the project.

When it comes to creating a grant proposal, this is one of the most critical aspects, since prospective funders will be looking for assessments.

It doesn't matter if we're talking about private or public foundations when we say this: each one of them has to know whether or not the program in which they funded made a difference.

Evaluations may be extremely pricey and are required to include admission and exit criteria as well as actions that are precisely targeted within the evaluation's scope. Due to the fact that this phase has a high potential for budget overruns, it is imperative that any actions outside the purview of the review be stated.

Again, a sound discipline and methodology for project management will retain a good emphasis on the evaluation tasks and outcomes.

Do:

Get people's opinions: No matter how you envision your assessment method, it is imperative that it incorporate some kind of input from the community that is participating in the project.

Make a choice between an internal evaluation and an outside review: In this situation, one of the most crucial factors to consider is whether or not the assessment will be carried out by your team or by an external organization that will conduct it independently.

Don't:

You can't afford to be specific: you need to provide a detailed explanation of the measuring techniques that will inform you and your sponsors how well the program is functioning. No room for ambiguities here.

Ignore the various time frames: It is not enough to just measure achievement; rather, one must measure success over an extended period of time. Therefore, you should make sure that your evaluation techniques include regular intervals.

To return to our earlier example of teaching reading to children, the following is how an evaluation of that effort may look:

Project Evaluation

Students will take a series of pre-tests and post-tests that will be administered by program facilitators in order to evaluate the degree to which the project is meeting its goals. The periodic examinations will be formulated by a group of external collaborators who are specialists in the field of child education, and they will be carried out on a monthly basis for the entirety of the program.

We will invite the participating instructors to provide a qualitative assessment at the end of each session in order to identify areas of development and generate feedback

Step 8: Alternative sources of finance and long-term viability

Your company's founders probably won't go for the concept of investing in a project that has no vision and only a short time horizon. They will be far more inclined to acknowledge a winner over the long term and reward an encouraging project that can be implemented on a wider scale.

Because of this, you need to demonstrate how you can make this happen in some way.

This portion of your grant submission is for the financing requirements that extend beyond the scope of the project, such as the total cost of ownership, which includes the cost of ongoing maintenance, everyday operations, and operational support.

It is possible that you may be required to detail the ongoing costs that are anticipated (if any) over a period of at least 5 years.

For a cost model to be correct, all relevant aspects, such as inflation, specialized skills, continuous training, possible future growth, and decommissioning charges (incurred when a project or product reaches the end of its life cycle), need to be accounted for.

Do:

Make sure you have a solid plan: Because the majority of grant evaluators have some

43

experience with business strategies, it is imperative that you present a workable strategy for long-term sustainability. How exactly do you intend to make money off of your endeavor and keep it moving forward?

Mention any other sources of funding: This is the spot to state that you intend to seek extra funds from the government, if that is the case. Do not be under the impression that this is not a viable plan for the long run.

Don't:

If there is anything else: Do not leave any room for supposition or for the reader to fill in the spaces. Everything has to be laid out, and you have to demonstrate without a shadow of a doubt that your software can continue operating long after the initial resources have been depleted.

Step 9: Outline a budget for the project.

Budgeting is, without a doubt, one of the most significant subjects that may be included in grant proposals. At this point in the process, you should go into specifics of exactly how you will put the available resources to use from a logistical aspect.

Please provide a detailed justification for all costs, including a table of services (or service catalog) and products supplied, which may be used to explain the services in a manner that is both clear and accurate.

Keep in mind that the most important part of your grant submission is the section on the project's budget.

If you overcharge for your services or provide a high price, you risk not only losing the grant but also being perceived as profiteering. If you underbid your competition, you could win the business, but you run the risk of being unable to deliver on the promises made in your proposal, which could damage your relationship with the grantee.

A significant number of grantors underquote with the anticipation of "hooking" the reader and subsequently searching for extra financing at a later point.

Playing this risky game might have a negative impact on your personal or corporate brand, as well as your status in the community and reputation in your sector.

Do:

Pay attention to detail: It is necessary to ensure that everything, and we do mean everything, is covered. Be sure to include in everything, including the cost of travel, supplies, advertising, and people.

Double-check: Accidentally throwing off the whole calculation by omitting a zero or moving the decimal point can be surprisingly simple. Make every effort!

Don't forget to round your numbers: This is purely for the benefit of the audience. It will be more difficult to keep track of the situation if there are a lot of decimal points and uneven figures.

Don't:

Do it alone: Don't be afraid to bring in other individuals and put together a group to work on this project with you. This is especially important if you're not very good with figures.

Put indirect expenses out of your mind: A significant number of grant writers will exclude ancillary expenditures such as insurance, utility bills, garbage collection, and so on. These may quickly become a burden, so watch out that you don't forget about them!

THE END